Finding Lions Among Lambs

How to Create a Performance Culture and Locate Top Millennial Talent

The Guru Leadership Series

By Jack Diaz

Welcome to The Guru Leadership Series

For great free content and additional information, email us at **ask@whatthegurusays.com**.

Or

Join us on Facebook at What The Guru Says

At the end of the book, we have added some great tools to help you and your business, and to assist in teaching these concepts.

J. H. Dies retains the exclusive rights to any use and application or adaptation of this book

Finding Lions Among Lambs How to Create a Performance Culture and Locate Top Millennial Talent. Copyright© 2017 by J .H. Dies All rights reserved. Printed in the United States of America. No part of this book may be used or reproduced in any manner whatsoever without written permission except in the case of brief quotations embodied in critical articles and reviews.

FIRST EDITION

Library of Congress Cataloging in Publication data has been applied for

The Guru Mission

Our Mission is to improve businesses and their people with simple, actionable ideas.

This Guru Book

This book is intended to be read in an hour or so, and then revisited as a reference tool as needed.

One of the reasons companies struggle in maximizing the contribution and impact of employees is because they have not established a performance culture. Business leaders everywhere are crying out for talent, and bemoaning the absence of great employees from the stereotypical millennial masses.

The reality is that exceptional talent is there to be found, if the search is done well. A culture that emphasizes performance, once ingrained is contagious, and with maintenance, will launch the business that creates it forward.

Leadership has an impact on all of these problems. This book is designed to simplify how you think about performance, and who you should hire, but it is not intended to be a statistical analysis of employee time consumption.

Read it with a mind toward issue spotting, and use guru techniques to get more out of your employees, which will improve your profitability, and the quality of your talent.

Table of Contents

Section I Culture Creation

1. The Dog Died Question – Creating a Performance Culture...1

2. The Metrics Myth – Data and The Incomplete Panacea 13

3. Investment – The Most Underrated Culture Creator Ever...21

4. Transparency – Killing Gossip & Improving Performance...35

5. The Folly of Success – Maintaining Hunger After the Feast 47

Section II Locating Top Talent

6. Another Test? - Diagnosing Performers for Cloning 55

7. Stop Asking Bad Questions – Interviewing for Greatness...63

8. The Millennial Myth – Separating Hope from Hype..........73

9. What Good Are Caged Lions? –Teaching Your New Talent to Lead 81

10. What do They Say? - Millennials in Their Own Words….....93

Chapter 1
The My Dog Died Question -

"Performance, and performance alone, dictates the predator in any food chain." - SEAL Team saying

Some time ago, a leader I very much admire gathered his lieutenants together to ask a question that goes to the heart of top performing cultures.

The scenario went like this:

Employee X walks into your office, and says, "My dog died, and I need a week off." As the team lead, you may ask one question, and only one. What do you ask, and why? What actions do you take while you are interacting with the employee, and after the discussion?

At the time, I had already been a part of a true high performance culture for some time, and to some degree took that for granted. My answer was typical.

I said, "I would ask what work he or she had on her plate, requesting thoughts on how we could find coverage, and decide on the approach based upon that answer."

And boy did I get the answer wrong.

There were many variations on my theme, and others gave different answers. Some digressed and dove into the issue of how important a pet can be to a family, but in this room of very smart people, none of us got close.

After watching us struggle with this for some time, the leader looked at all of us and asked the very simple question. "Is this person a high performer?" The answer to that question will tell you everything you need to know.

The true weight of high performers in a meritocracy cannot be overstated. Employees deserve professionalism and respect, and unfair treatment based on race, religion, age or disability is not just reprehensible. It is illegal. That said, the notion that everyone should be treated equally with regard to rewards, privileges, or compensation is a cancerous proposition that must be discarded before a high performance culture is possible. Not only should you be exaggerating your efforts to reward performers, you should do so very publicly.

What is a High Performance Culture?

A high performance culture is a business environment characterized by meritocracy, where performance is openly defined and measured, and where compensation, advancement, and bonuses/perks are disproportionately awarded to those who have succeeded at the highest levels.

Each organization may have variation as to how performance and high performance are defined, but there are aspects of this definition that are fixed, and which must exist before an organization can be deemed to have a high performance culture.

First, performance must be largely objectively identifiable. Whether that be sales numbers measured in the form of revenue, indicia of productivity such as projects completed in a service environment, or convictions at a District Attorney's office, people in the organization need to be readily aware of how performance is measured. Metrics are not a panacea, and that will be discussed in the next chapter, but if used correctly, they can be a useful diagnostic tool for measuring aspects of performance.

Second, performance of the team must be clear to its members. The word transparency has been thrown around to the point of becoming a cliché, but for high performance cultures team members must be aware of where they stand relative to each other. This is true for a number of reasons. A mediocre employee who believes they are a top performer will not get better. A struggling employee who wants to get better needs to know who to emulate in the organization to advance. Finally, when rewards are bestowed, this clarity is required to avoid the appearance of subjective favoritism, and unfair treatment of employees.

The last tenant of a high performance culture is its tendency to reward and celebrate true performers. This can and should be done with compensation, (whether that is higher commissions or bonuses), advancement (in both title and importance to the organization), and with positive attention that celebrates the exploits of these employees in front of their peers. It is critically important when these huge rewards are passed out, or special considerations are given, that the message to the group at large be very clear as to what this performer did to get the bonus or recognition, and that such rewards are available to all who perform similarly.

A consulting firm might publicly award a huge check to the team member that has the most referrals from current clients. Some companies have exclusive "clubs" consisting of top performers who are entitled to perks, time off, trips, gym or golf memberships etcetera. Our firm has used a number of these, in addition to personal training sessions in the gym and other "treats." In each case we monitor how perks are received both by those to whom they are awarded, and by the number of questions we get from others about what it takes to qualify for such awards. To be truly effective both sides of that equation must be in place.

Finally, high performance cultures distinguish between themselves, and time and tenure firms from the moment they meet a prospective employee. They celebrate the fact that promotions and raises come more quickly for those who engage and perform. This does two things. It entices the right kind of employee into the environment, and when employed for some time, serves as a constant reminder to that employee that time spent with the firm is valued, but that metaphorical resting in performance will slow advancement and rewards.

The Paradox of Performers

Many law firms, large accounting firms, government entities, and businesses (especially large ones), have a time and tenure pecking order. One must be at the firm eight years to be eligible for a particular promotion, or partnership by way of example. This lack of meritocracy will systematically remove a disproportionate number of high performers from the organization, and replace them with much more mediocre counterparts.

The paradox works thusly:

The high performer is recognized quickly for his or her abilities to put together exceptional work product, create client relationships, or generate revenue. Medium to low performers are noticed for their abilities to provide passable, and maybe even unacceptable work, requiring more oversight or effort by the delegator.

A natural, and frankly intelligent, bias forms such that good or important work is pushed to the high performer, while less or no work goes to the high performer's peers. The performer is intelligent enough to recognize both that she is doing better work, and more work, but also that she is in precisely the same line for promotions, raises etc., as the medium to low performers. Resentment forms, and the high performer leaves.

Meanwhile, since little to no pressure, and a materially lighter workload are pushed on the low/medium performers, they are happy to wait out the promotion track in collective mediocrity. Suddenly the workplace is lacking in precisely the employees needed to make it great, and the company's trajectory stagnates.

Consider the alternative. If extra praise, bonuses, compensation, and promotions were transparently heaped on the high performer, the medium low performers are encouraged and incentivized to model the rewarded behavior. If they believe they are entitled to equal treatment regardless of personal contribution, and unwilling to improve their contributions, the low and medium performers, perceiving a lack of fairness, may take themselves out of the equation altogether. In either case the company wins over time, because the system is actively creating achievers and discouraging or culling non-achievers.

This is not to say that companies with too many low or non-performers should immediately slash and burn the workforce. However, the system created by the organization should be automatically honed to reward performance without the need for individuals to do so on an ad hoc basis. This is critical in high growth environments, and growth is a given in true high performance business environments.

The qualification for, and completion of awards should be well understood by all, tied to objective criteria, and consistently followed through to ensure that there is no appearance of favoritism.

Ad hoc, or situational bonuses, and awards are fine, and occasionally they serve to encourage emphasis on finer points of company goals, while boosting morale, but if awards are not consistent or predictable, they will be materially less effective in driving behavior.

So what does all of this have to do with the "my dog died," question?

If the employee coming to leadership with the request for a week off is a high performer, they will have seen to it that work was covered, clients were taken care of, and business was handled. Frankly even if they didn't, leadership should go out of the way to make the environment hospitable for top performers. Granting this accommodation impacts engagement, and further solidifies the relationship between company and performer. The reverse is also true. Failure to accommodate such requests damages the relationship between company and performer, the consequences of which should not be taken lightly.

If the employee is a low performer, the issue is not the death of the pet. It is their contribution. The likelihood that time bombs and other issues will surface in the employee's absence is quite good. This is the employee who has flat tires several times a month, and a myriad of reasons why they simply cannot perform at the expected level. Grief in the loss of a pet is just the newest of those.

The broader application of this principle is that leadership is constantly being asked to make decisions about the allocation of resources, and benefits. When an employee asks to deviate from company policy, or seeks a benefit, reward, or other incentive, leadership should weigh that person's contribution in deciding whether to accommodate. The single criteria should be the lens offered from the question, "Is this person a high performer?" This doesn't mean leaving better judgment at the door, but if your employees see special rules, privileges, and treatment extended to high performers, they will seek to immolate them, and your business will be richly rewarded.

A number of fantastic companies have an "unlimited vacation," policy for high performers. It is not that they expect these employees to take off forever. It is that these employees will only take off when their responsibilities have been handled, and/or they absolutely need to. Frankly, we find ourselves pushing performers out the door to take personal time, because too often they run the risk of wearing themselves out for failing to take any time at all.

When it comes to rewards, be public about it, and more will follow. This is not simply preferential treatment. It is mindful, transparent preferential treatment, designed to create desired behaviors.

Chapter 2. The Metrics Myth - Data and the Incomplete Panacea

"What's measured improves." – Peter F. Drucker

The massive proliferation of easily available data has revolutionized business. Companies who use data intelligently have a massive advantage over their casual data use counterparts. Having observed this phenomenon, business have in some cases abandoned prudence, choosing instead to be governed by spreadsheets.

To be clear, data has its place in all good business. As discussed in Chapter 1, the importance of objectivity in defining high performance cannot be understated. On the other hand, data without proper analysis can be a gun pointed in the wrong direction.

It is this fundamental truth that makes Drucker's quote much more complex than it appears. Consider a consulting firm that suddenly announces that it will begin to track billable hours on a per employee or per team basis. Drucker's statement is correct that billable hours will improve (at least in terms of the number of hours). That cannot be where the analysis ends. It is not enough that billable hours go up, without further thought.

For example, if billable hours are up, because the extra scrutiny is causing people to more accurately or contemporaneously enter time, so that real time work has not been lost or forgotten, there is a win. If billable hours go up because unscrupulous employees are dishonestly padding time, you have a (potentially very damaging) loss.

Consider the situation of a local restaurant. The location was very successful, and had a bar that was lucrative both for the restaurant, and the bartenders who were well compensated in tips. The manager needed another bartender, and given the history of the restaurant to hire bartenders from within, he decided to offer a contest.

The waiter with the highest liquor, beer, and wine sales as a percentage of total sales was to be the new bartender, under the assumption that this waiter would be the most adept with knowledge of the product and encouraging guests to purchase alcoholic beverages. The waiter with the highest percentage of alcohol sales beat his competition handily by more than a double digit margin as compared to his next closest competitor.

When asked how, the waiter replied, "I would get the guests to order their first round of drinks, and upon delivering them I would advise the guest of our free happy hour food offerings which were quite good. When the guest closed the tab, I had a 100% alcohol sale. I reasoned that in the short term I would earn less tips this way, but upon reaching the bar I would more than make up for it."

Nothing this waiter did was "cheating," but by emphasizing one metric to the exclusion of reason, the restaurant ironically encouraged one of its bestselling waiters to actually undermine the fundamental goals of the business.

That result may seem absurd, but it happens all the time, when companies blindly apply metrics to problems without further inquiry. Every metric is subject to misinterpretation, and the potential to confuse or confound a business' goals. Pure productivity metrics, when emphasized poorly can lead to a decrease of quality. Client satisfaction metrics without scrutiny can be manipulated by fast talking employees who convince customers to answer at higher satisfaction levels than the customer actually felt.

This situation is further complicated when the data is shared with teams publicly as a means of inspiring competition, or to provide clarity as to where team members stand relative to each other. A number of intelligent business writers have suggested that publicly sharing metrics can create hostility in workers toward each other, and have a net negative effect.

We see this as an oversimplification. If an organization creates a supportive environment, and mindful messaging is used within teams, openly sharing data can be remarkably constructive and helpful in improving team performance.

Trouble starts where messaging is off, fostering hostility, or where there is no buy-in from the team as to either the reliability of the metric (or data), or the inference that can be drawn from it. Under these circumstances, publicly rewarding a winner can actually cause harm.

Consider the previous restaurant example. How should otherwise competent hard working wait staff react to the promotion of one of their peers, who actively encouraged patrons not to buy food? Now, what was otherwise set up to be the positive celebration of a high performing employee, becomes cancerous, undermines confidence in leadership, and fosters a general sense of unfairness in the troops.

This is not an endorsement for the abandonment of metrics. To the contrary, data for example on the most effective leads in terms of closures and revenue may push a sales team to change its focus in magnificent ways. Instead, we would advocate for constructive wariness of metrics and the inferences that can be drawn from them.

Growing young companies are particularly challenged in this regard. A very talented, if small, nucleus of leaders can be very effective in driving change and growth in a small organization. As the group grows, the ability to observe employees, influence individual performance, and keep up with the wild growth of new information into the company can become unwieldy. There is temptation to rely too heavily on metrics, which if unartfully done, results in poor decision making. Suddenly a vibrant small company with real trajectory becomes a sluggish middle sized firm that has lost its way.

Metrics should be seen as a sword for the business that should be constantly sharpened. Mindful examination of factors that could skew the data, or unsupported assumptions based on blind spots in the data must be vigorously sought out. Leadership should interact with the staff to discuss how to refine metrics, and to affirm buy in as to the conclusions to be drawn from it.

In that environment, metrics are constructive tools that teach people where they stand relative to each other, while allowing teams to share in the excitement of real time vision into the growth of the firm.

One effective means of tracking the effectiveness of metric data is a performer calibration meeting. Team leads are brought together to discuss performance. Without access to the most up to date data, the leads are asked to rank in order, their performers highest to lowest, and to achieve as much consensus as possible. When all agree on the rankings, or get as close as is possible, metrics are introduced to see if the data supports the group's conclusions as to performance. The company should not assume that in the case of discrepancy, it is the judgment of team leads that is wrong. While that is certainly possible, close scrutiny of the reliability of the metrics must also be taken into consideration to ensure that the tools are working.

Another fun variation on this approach is to do a draft in the way that pro sports teams do, followed by a discussion of which players were chosen by the leads, and why. Upon completion of the discussion, performance data is introduced to corroborate or spur further evaluation of these conclusions.

Both of these exercises are incredibly effective at encouraging constructive dialogue aimed toward consistency in leadership as to how the team is evaluated. They also provide opportunities for rigorous investigation of confirmation bias and the other challenges that regularly confront good leaders.

Chapter 3. Investment - The Most Underrated Culture Creator Ever

"Customers will never love a company until the employees love it first." – Simon Sinek

Hundreds of hours of the time of brilliant business minds have been spent discussing corporate culture and the shared set of values that a successful company must pass on to its people.

There are certainly a number of great ones. Teamwork, ownership, urgency, accountability, energy, passion, performance, and many other values are likely to come up in such conversations. If you seek a true performance culture, there is one which must be paramount, and that value is investment.

Investment in this context is used in precisely the same way that it is used financially, with the mindful allocation of resources and the goal that they will grow at the most advantageous pace possible. The only difference is that the capital invested here is human capital. Employees are taught from the outset, that the company wants its customers to have an extraordinary experience in their interactions with the business. The organization then explains its belief that this is only possible where employees feel valued and invested in, such that their passion for the organization is passed on to customers.

Two Faces of Investment

For investment to work, new employees and leadership must have an early, common understanding of expectations.

The first of the two faces of investment relates to the investment expectations for leadership in a performance culture. Performance leaders create relationships with their subordinates that foster a connectivity, characterized by the employee's genuine belief that the leader has the employee's best interest at heart. Performance leadership comes from a place of service, not power. The subject of leadership as an act of service is discussed in some detail later in the book.

It is not enough that the leader and employee have this relationship. The performance leader must leverage that relationship to get the most from the employee, thus advancing the talents and career of the employee while advancing the interests of the company. The performance leader strikes an appropriate balance between celebrating accomplishment, and creating constructive tension where employee performance lags behind potential.

Good leaders must have the ability to forge these relationships, but even the best of these connections takes time. For that reason considerable detail should be placed in to who the company selects for leadership, what successes a leader has achieved in creating other leaders, and the individual match of a particular new employee with the mentor to whom the employee will be entrusted.

A performance culture facilitates these relationships by creating an alignment of interests, which fosters cooperation. For example, new employees should be advised from the beginning that both the employee and the leader will be judged by that employee's success in achieving goals and/or securing promotion. In this way, the company creates a commonality that can be built upon quickly.

Performance cultures judge the effectiveness of leaders both by their ability to achieve high performance in employees, and by the ability to develop those employees into leaders themselves. Investment is the mechanism by which this is achieved. Similarly, in instances where an employee is performing disappointingly, the organization must judge leaders by their ability to objectively diagnose the situation, and remedy it, or counsel out the employees that are not capable of succeeding in the organization. This latter ability is critical to ensure that important resources are not invested in those who cannot reasonably be expected to ascend to the ranks of high performers.

New employees should see the organization's willingness to spend time and resources toward the employee's advancement. This occurs with guidance through training, constant objective feedback, and clarity as to the path required for advancement of the employee as well as regular calibration on remaining steps required for advancement with agreed timelines. Employees should be readily able to explain their own specific performance goals, and remaining milestones for promotion.

Lastly on this first face of investment, employees should be actively encouraged to provide feedback, both directly to their leaders, and in the event of disagreement, to the leader's supervisor. If messaging is handled properly, and the right kind of relationship exists between leader and employee, the employee understands that there is trust among leadership, and so long as feedback is constructive, it will be openly welcomed. This is not a function of "ratting," on a supervisor. Rather, it is a reflection of a shared organizational belief that all members of the team can improve and grow, with a common honest desire to do so including leaders.

Such an environment encourages employees to hold leadership accountable in the same way that leadership is expected to hold subordinates accountable. The effect is a kind of automation, where all involved are pushing each other to get better. This notion is entirely awkward to the typical incoming employee. Many are conditioned never to criticize or speak "ill" of their leaders or bosses. It is critical that a distinction be drawn between toxic negativity, and constructive feedback.

Further, the organization must foster a sort of social contract that those receive constructive criticism will do so without undo defensiveness. The fastest way to kill constructive tension, and the feedback necessary for growth if defensiveness. The most seasoned of talent developers will eventually quit push people who make criticism personal, or who react overly emotionally to the proposition that they could be better, faster, or stronger. Companies that deal with defensiveness directly will prosper. This is because employees see that a proper tone is taken in listening to and acting on constructive feedback, by all involved. If there is a feeling of retribution by those in leadership for radical candor in employees, such feedback will disappear quickly.

The second face of investment relates to the employees expected investment in their own careers, and by extension into the company.

Performance cultures work hard, very early in the new employee development process to get excited about the opportunity presented by the position at the firm. These cultures encourage tenacious effort to absorb, and work on applying the new material as quickly as possible. A robust training program is a must, and clear expectations on participation, pre-training material review etc., must be laid out clearly.

Emphasizing the return to be reaped from a strong effort in that 90-120 period beginning a new post, drives employees to push. This coupled with the typical excitement of a new job, should get most of them on the right track. Simple things like post training follow-up on the morning after an evening training session with the mentor will ensure that confusion or questions get addressed, and that the new employee is prepared and paying attention both for class, and for the meeting to discuss class the next day.

As the employee develops, and skills improve, the discussions about what is expected in terms of employee investment in the firm should evolve. In the initial phases, performance cultures will do their part to emphasize the commitment of mentors and trainers to invest in new employees to get them to the next level. As employees reach mastery, the ask changes to a pay it forward mentality, which helps newcomers on the very same journey. One of the greatest tools for transitioning new employees, and evaluating leadership potential in recent mastery employees is informally pairing those 6-12 month employees with newcomers, while the experience of new arrival to the company is fresh in the mentor's head.

Performance cultures do other things from an investment standpoint, to show employees how they are valued by the organization. These range from expensive, free food, gyms, and or a robust wellness program, to inexpensive, with company sponsored time off FOR HIGH PERFORMERS, to allow them to give back to their communities through membership in charitable causes. The importance of these kinds of incentives is paramount for millennials as addressed below, but these rewards are impactful for employees of all experience levels and ages.

In his study with the Case Foundation, Derrick Feldman argued that the millennial generation looks to direct managers, for opportunities to make a difference, and participate in what he calls "company cause work." Such projects provide a sense of fulfillment that was less important to their predecessors as a whole, but which materially impacts job satisfaction for this new generation.

This work outside the office, and a clear message about the good a company provides in terms of giving back to its clients, its community, and the economy as a whole are all important to workers. Finally, the notion that a company would listen to its lowest tenured employees, and act on what is important to them, gives these employees a strong sense of investment.

These opportunities also strengthen the organization through improving local ties, and positive brand recognition that helps with clients, and important organizational relationships.

What to Tell Your Leaders about Investment

Companies tend to place great pressure on their leaders to achieve team performance goals, keep employee retention rates up, execute on company mission items, and cultivate new talent through their ranks. All of this is important, but none of it is as important as investment.

Mary Blitzer Field, in her work on leadership, has identified four primary leadership styles. She breaks them down as follows:

- The Direct Leader – take charge style capable of pulling teams through crisis
- The Spirited Leader – uses spontaneity to create a vital spark in flagging team energy
- The Considerate Leader – creates unity though team harmony getting performance through loyalty
- The Systematic Leader – applies analytical talents to maximize team results.

None of these styles is said to be inherently better than any other style, and most leaders employ some combination of each of these styles naturally. It is rare for any one leader to comfortably apply any of the four styles with equal dexterity, but many good leaders will have strong skills in two or more of these approaches.

Identifying where your leaders are on this spectrum is important in a performance culture, because not all of these styles carry the requisite empathy to successfully create an emphasis on investment. It is in fact quite important that an effective leader have the natural ability to exercise empathy when called for on his or her team.

There are a number of different studies that have concluded that the number one reason a person leaves their job is a poor relationship/experience with their direct supervisor.

Investment is designed to counter this phenomenon. When employees believe that their company and their supervisor genuinely care about them as people, and about their advancement professionally, other concerns such as compensation, demands of work during busy times, and on the job stress are easily overcome.

This is not to say that investment gives any company license to under compensate employees. To the contrary, in a performance culture, top employees are paid above market, and that is made known to them. However, the bond created where the chemistry of investment is concerned allows for an openness to addressing matters such as compensation, advancement, and frustrations with the work that often drive employees away. In addition, the typical employee who has this kind of relationship with a mentor will have a much harder time leaving the organization over a few dollars, or the unproven promise of a shinier job.

Chapter 4. Transparency – Killing Gossip and Improving Performance

"I've come to learn there is a virtuous cycle to transparency and a very vicious cycle of obfuscation." – Jeff Weiner

Few corporate values create more fear and confusion than transparency. Performance cultures simply cannot exist without it. Ironically, transparency is a corporate buzzword thrown around constantly in an attempt to inspire confidence or security in environments that are not the least bit transparent.

For many companies true transparency can be incredibly difficult to create. In companies that struggle with transparency, there is always a single cause. Failure of leadership in exhibiting and embracing these behaviors will guarantee that a company is not transparent.

Before we dive into how to foster transparency and leverage it in creating a high performance culture, we should define transparency clearly.

Transparency is constructive honesty aimed at bettering the firm and its people.

Transparency is not brutal directness for its own sake, and everything that is true need not always be said.

Proper honesty, and motivation are critical to fostering the appropriate kind of transparency in an organization. To be clear, transparency can and often should be uncomfortable. A huge challenge for new leaders arises in creating the constructive tension required for maximum performance. Similarly, to be effective, transparency must be well timed.

Consider the close friend who advises that you shouldn't wear a particular outfit because it is unflattering. This kind of honesty can be uncomfortable, but among friends, and family it is commonplace and often accepted with nothing more than friendly banter. The key distinction here is that the honesty comes from a source that is both loyal, and an unquestionable advocate for the bests interests of the person being advised.

It would be rude or worse for someone unknown to provide the same advice on an unflattering outfit, even though the content of the communication could be identical.

In its most impactful form, transparency takes the shape of a healthy marital relationship, the close sibling ties, or best friends who have shared a lifetime of treasured experiences. These folks are unfailingly honest, and always coming from a place of support. For some reason, business relationships and the pretext of professionalism often create boundaries that frustrate the purposes of transparency.

Companies know their employees are closely knit when they spend time together, even when they don't have to. The organizations that foster the intense competition, and support that mirrors the competitiveness of elite sports organizations will see a natural symmetry between their employees that is absolutely transparent.

For leaders, building and fostering this relationship through consistent support and investment is the only way to get to a place where transparency can exist openly. Even then, for true transparency to take root, the desire to share constructive information must be even handed, and embraced whether it comes from subordinate to supervisor or vice versa. Particularly in the beginning, transparency will be fragile.

Overbearing, or overly confident leadership that takes a condescending tone when confronted with disagreement or constructive criticism, will chill honest feedback from team members, stifling growth.

Leadership may only receive constructive feedback in one of two ways to facilitate and encourage ongoing transparency.

In circumstances where the leader disagrees with the feedback or proposed course, leadership owes the dissenter a thoughtful, well-reasoned response articulating the basis for disagreement (preferably while contemporaneously expressing appreciation for the dissent). Sometimes this response should be public. For example, if a team member raises a concern or area of disagreement that others may share, a good leader may thank the person for the feedback, and raise it with the team, hoping to facilitate a great discussion. This fosters buy in from the team, and if ultimately the leader is called to make a decision to move in another direction, none can say the argument wasn't fairly heard.

In circumstances where the leader believes there is merit, or even an actionable basis for changing company protocol upon receiving constructive feedback, the leader must celebrate the idea privately and publicly, while encouraging others to provide feedback. One great predictor of high growth innovative brands is their tendency to embrace change and ideas. Your high performance culture must do this to succeed.

The Challenge of Public Transparency

One of the most challenging contexts for fostering transparency involves the public sharing of constructive criticism. There is a tendency to hold that any constructive criticism of an employee should only involve that employee, and only be dispensed privately. We believe this is wrong.

As with anything, there are exceptions. If a person is dealing with a highly personal and private problem, and that problem is impacting performance or worse, a leader may have to take up that issue privately. A common example of this would be health problems.

On the other hand, sharing challenges facing particular individuals even publicly can very positively impact performance in an organization. Tone and delivery are key, and it must always be clear to all involved that feedback is coming from a place of trying to help the recipient be bigger, faster, or stronger.

An example of this common to performance cultures is the use of mocks, or simulated real life practice rounds. These can occur in the context of client interactions, overcoming objections, practicing a decision matrix, diagnosing problems and more.

If mocks are done publicly, and correctly, the performance and skill of the team will be materially accelerated.

Here is how:

The leader sets up a mock where he or she plays a customer frustrated by some problem, and invites a team member to be the employee confronted by this customer. The two go through a dialogue wherein the employee tries to solve the problem, calm the customer and save the day.

At a reasonable point, the leader breaks the fiction, and beginning with the newest team members asks them for constructive feedback on the exchange. The leader progresses to more senior team members who provide their feedback, and the leader finishes with closing thoughts.

This type of mock scenario with transparent feedback is helpful on many levels. First, newer team members get to see these situations, and decide what if anything they would have done differently. Upon feedback from senior team members and the leader, all learn the best technique.

Moreover, the leader is given the opportunity to assess not just the person in the mock, but the instincts of all on the team, as to how they pick up on strengths and weaknesses of the approach used in the exercise. It is important to start with lesser experienced team members, as they are likely to be influenced by more senior teammates if senior thoughts are expressed first. Finally, in welcoming feedback in a group setting, the leaders are modeling the behaviors they expect of the group.

Criticism in a public setting is something that many companies and leaders struggle with, though often the struggle is unnecessary. It is common to use the "sandwich approach," when providing feedback, where the critic starts and finishes with compliments on what was done well, or a strength of the employee, sandwiching between those things suggestions on areas of improvement.

There is nothing wrong with this per se, but a performance organization where members are conditioned on the benefits of constructive feedback, doesn't require artificial niceties. Moreover, the truly constructive feedback, which is most important anyway is not confused between two pieces of extraneous information.

High performance cultures condition their employees to be comfortable receiving such criticism, and prepare leaders for how and when to deliver it. Messaging and tone are critical when this feedback is shared, and context is everything, but if a team knows where its members are struggling, and where they are succeeding, the team is better equipped to help itself to improve.

Performance organizations prepare new employees for transparency, and even vet prospective employees on the issue of how they take criticism. We regularly ask candidates for constructive criticism they have received, and the employee's response to it. It is easy to tell when a person recounts having received constructive feedback, whether that person is comfortable in that setting.

The benefits of transparency in a performance culture are numerous. First, the speed of development is greatly accelerated because the employee is given real time feedback on how to improve at every opportunity, rather than waiting for an annual or semiannual review.

Second, gossip and concerns about favoritism fade away, because the group sees where all of its members stand relative to each other. In environments where criticism is only offered behind closed doors, there is a natural tendency to focus inward such that each employee believes they are the only one being criticized. Finally, there is the benefit of the influence of the group to help lift areas of weakness, and reinforce the need to constantly strive for improvement.

One of the reasons that the military and sports teams are so well recognized for their ability to improve through competitive achievement is that they constantly use positive peer pressure to create constructive tension to improve weaker teammates.

The individual feels obligated not to let the team down, and pushes to perform at a higher level, while the team drives each other at every turn. In sports, and in the military, deficiencies might be more openly obvious to the group, who can easily see performance weaknesses. In performance cultures, leadership will air these concerns, and encourage the team to help, until the team begins to do so by itself. In so doing, the rising tide carries all.

Your typical employees and even many of your leadership will be uncomfortable with constructive tension. Performance cultures push through this discomfort, actively seeking opportunities to confront until it becomes second nature. Without this tension, employees will never perform beyond their own perceived potential.

Senior leadership should occasionally attend the meetings of junior team leads to ensure that constructive tension exists. Through the asking of thought provoking questions that force participation, that dive deep into the true thoughts of the team, while confronting any absence of candor, the senior leader will model behaviors required for organizational success.

Chapter 5. The Folly of Success – Maintaining Hunger after the Feast.

The question isn't who is going to let me; it's who is going to stop me – Ayn Rand

The entrepreneur's folly goes something like this: Be hungry. Be passionate. Be single mindedly focused on the achievement of your goals. Achieve the goals. Lose sight of what caused that success, and lose it all.

This journey is almost cliché for newly founded businesses. In the beginning, it is very easy to focus on the details, and what will make the business work with the unique contributions of its founder. Starting a successful business is the easy part. Keeping a business growing is much more challenging.

In my work with a number of incredibly successful business founders, I have encountered a number of different personalities with different individual talents and backgrounds, but one single characteristic was common to all of them. Each steadfastly refused to recognize their own past achievements with anything more than a passing nod.

These individuals have accumulated hundreds of millions of dollars of personal net worth in industries ranging from consulting, to real estate, to law. Each told stories of how their goals changed over time (one wanted to own real estate over 100 million dollars in value and did, another wanted to create a unicorn - business that went from startup to a billion dollar valuation, and did).

The thing that was common to all of them was that the moment they achieved these goals, the goals changed as though they had never been goals in the first place. Instead of asking "what do we need to do to get to a billion dollar brand," the question became "why are we not a three or four billion dollar brand?"

High performance cultures constantly focus on raising the bar in virtually every aspect of the business. They counter the very natural human tendency to bask in the success of an achievement, by pushing for that record to be broken. This doesn't mean that these cultures fail to celebrate the work of those who break a new sales record for example. It does mean that on January 1, the sole question is "who can beat the new record?"

The constant push to hire more talented people, improve product quality, enhance the customer experience, speed up the development process, and otherwise improve efficiency in an organization is necessary to keep the company hungry enough to get to the next level. In the next chapter we will discuss hiring with particularity, but the mechanism by which organizations keep this "hunger" must be discussed.

The how can be summed up in one word. Disruption. The notion that if a thing isn't broken, it shouldn't be fixed is absolutely poisonous to the ongoing growth of a high performance culture. At the time this book is being written Sears has publicly expressed grave concerns about its financial survival. Consider the parable that this and many other companies like it can teach us.

In its origin, Sears was a massively disruptive brand. It changed the fundamental way that consumers purchased goods. A number of highly successful local stores slowly died in the presence of a brand that could sell a world full of goods to anyone holding its catalogue.

Another example of this phenomenon was Nokia. Despite a more than 125 year old reputation for innovation, it was not until the 1990's that Nokia truly dominated a global market. During this period, Motorola and a number of other cell phone maker's simply couldn't master the blend of functionality and consumer friendliness that Nokia achieved. People didn't event speak in terms of the name of their phone maker. They simply called their phones by a model number. Then Nokia got complacent. In January of 2007, Steve Jobs pulled an iphone from his pocket, changed the world, and reduced a globally dominant brand to the annals of history.

These are not isolated instances, and examples of incredible growth tell the opposite story. Consider Amazon, Google, and Facebook. Each of these brands grew massive incredibly quickly, based on a formula of constant disruption. That which was assumed to be the case was thrown out in favor of thoughtful experiments.

These companies have embraced and encouraged disruption as a part of their cultures. The notion that the author of an idea is not nearly so important as the quality of an idea seems obvious, but companies continue to chill innovation in favor of "what we have always done."

The challenge of disruption is that success haunts it. When a new technique, or sales approach achieves relative success, the natural human tendency is to try to emulate it. High performance cultures balance the high wire of recognizing and chronicling achievement, with a constant mindful eye of weaknesses or new approaches.

The companies that ask "what is wrong with what we are doing?" or "what are the fair criticisms of our product or service?" have a much better chance of thriving into the future than their counterparts who assume the journey has been mastered.

High performance cultures have a humility that respects innovation in even their newest employees, and a welcoming candor that opens up people who have been conditioned not to recommend change. These organizations constantly celebrate innovation by not only recognizing those with new ideas, but rewarding them in a public way that is proportionate to the value of their idea to the company.

Leaders of these companies have a coaching mentality that constantly pushes. They acknowledge that the group is getting better, while reminding that its adversaries are too.

Chapter 6. Another Test? – Diagnosing Performers for Cloning and Who Should Teach Them.

Teaching is the only major occupation of man for which we have not yet developed tools that make an average person capable of competence and performance. In teaching we rely on the 'naturals', the ones who somehow know how to teach. – Peter Drucker

The challenge of growth in an environment of constant change first requires identifying those who are driving the success of the company. This is often something metrics can isolate, but individual high performance is insufficient. The real work comes in the second step of separating those who can perform AND teach others how, from those whose highest and best use is to be lone wolves.

Companies very often drive away young lesser experienced high potential talent, by pairing it with impatient alphas, who are so far removed from the development process that they cannot even remember what it was like not to know how to do the work.

Landscapes of every sport, art, science and business are littered with the failures of those who achieved individually but cannot develop others.

High performance cultures must develop the ability to dispassionately isolate performers who can develop from those who cannot. Performance is often closely correlated to ego and self-image. Alphas often want the prestige associated with running a large team, and the elevated status and recognition that come with that.

Organizations with few true high performers, or those facing the 'give me a team,' demands of their best performers often find themselves held hostage in this setting.

In reality, this as an opportunity for an excellent conversation about what is required to get the privilege of developing others, and to use that as a mechanism to create real mentors. When an employee proves him or herself incapable of the true, often selfless work of helping others, a high performance culture recognizes this, placing the employee in the best possible positon for success. This may include pairing the employee with necessary support staff, and pushing for higher individual achievement.

But what if the employee quits? The simple answer here is that it is better to lose a single high performer than to constantly stifle the ability of rising talent to reach that status.

Reasonable diplomacy, and proper recognition for individual achievement can soften the blow of transparent recognition that not all high performers are mentors, but when faced with a 'give me a team or else,' mentality companies must have the strength to make the difficult decision.

So how do you identify those upon whose shoulders an army can be built, and the generals who will lead them?

A key component to replicating true needle movers in your organization is to use objective and subjective measures to isolate the characteristics of these folks that make them successful. This seems obvious, but the means by which organizations typically do this are often ineffective.

It is easy enough to notice things like technical preparation, work ethic, the ability to pivot, and other observable talents in members of a team. Similarly, technique and approaches that have been successful should be taught and replicated, but one of the most overlooked predictors of success in this arena is personal makeup.

There is no shortage of detractors in the world of personality makeup testing, but the reality is that successful organizations are increasingly relying upon these simple tests to determine fit for the organization and the role at issue.

The best and highest use of these instruments is to combine them with solid interview technique, to determine if the observations from the interview are consistent with the testing feedback. One of the most common corporate complaints about recruiting is the "professional interviewee," who shows up with a strong presentation that turns out not to be much of a reflection of the actual employee being hired.

There is a substantial body of work dedicated to accurately identifying the truth about who a prospective employee is, as opposed to the façade that a candidate may be trying to project.

Angela Duckworth, the author of Grit: The Power of Passion and Perseverance, has done incredible work in this regard. In particular, she looked at organizations that objectively demanded indisputable excellence of candidates, and still suffered substantial failure rates. An example she cites is West Point Academy, a school known for the highest academic, athletic, and leadership standards was still struggling with the number of graduates that completed the program.

Duckworth's research suggests that perseverance is grossly undervalued in determining the fit for those facing challenging environments. She created a test to diagnose perseverance, and that work, and her book are highly recommended as tools to assist with this particular challenge.

When attempting to replicate top talent in organizations, it makes sense to have the team's best and brightest take these surveys, and tally the results to see the traits common to those who perform at a high level in various departments within the organization.

The introspection alone can be worthwhile in reframing conceptions of common characteristics of top performers.

Some companies also use these tests with low performers to try to spot trends and/or characteristics they should avoid in seeking new candidates.

This analysis should be done both for lone wolves, and also for leaders and developers of talent. In the same way that average players can sometimes be exceptional coaches, results may paint a surprising picture of material differences in what works for the organization in distinguishing between successes individually, and developers of talent.

Chapter 7. Stop Asking Bad Questions – Interviewing for Greatness

Whenever you are asked if you can do a job, tell'em 'Certainly I can!' Then get busy and find out how to do it. – Theodore Roosevelt

If the interview is starting at the resume and not at a place of fundamentally understanding who the interviewee is, it is a failure. The best companies have already learned that if a remarkable talent is applying, the cutting edge company is much more interested in landing that talent for any viable role, than it is checking a box that matches a project description.

As a general rule, interviews are poorly done scripted questioning sessions, completed by poorly trained people, who have not spent real time preparing, for a mission critical task that is treated as mundane.

Good interviews should feel much more like casual conversations than interrogations, while still allowing for a deeper dive into who the candidate is and what motivates them. The idea is to have the person talk about themselves, their goals, and their interests, so that the interviewer can act as a lens into who the interviewee would fit into the organization, and the means by which that person is motivated.

An example question: Who do you most admire and why? The answer to this question will tell you a great deal about the candidate. If the question can't be answered reasonably fluidly and quickly, there is a very real chance that the interviewee has not taken the time to look for great examples to be emulated in reaching for goals, or worse, is unmotivated to achieve any goal beyond a 9-5 paycheck.

On the other hand, a well-considered response about a hardworking, innovative, or charismatic figure could provide great insights to the world view of the candidate.

Too much is made of specific qualification in terms of the skill required to do the job. This should be well vetted from the resume, and if the resume cannot clearly demonstrate requisite abilities, it is a reflection on the communication ability of the candidate that should work to exclude them before any interview takes place.

Performance focused organizations interview for passion, positivity, drive, and the ability to handle constructive tension and change. These companies regularly reject candidates that are objectively qualified for the job, where a candidate does not fit the team chemistry of the organization.

It is all well and good to say that interviews should be more about probing the individual, and less about resume box checking, but how is this properly accomplished?

Don't talk. At least not much. A great interview is an exercise in listening. Well considered questions will give the candidate much to expound upon. It is the reason I hate writing even one sample interview question such as the one above. The reader shouldn't come away with a list of 10 questions, although there are hundreds of great ones. A script will not serve. There should be many more "why's," "how's," and "tell me what you mean by that's."

The lost opportunity costs associated with investment in employees who don't make it, and the morale hit that comes from losing an employee who fails only after forming important relationships with co-workers, and clients will always exceed any upside of a bad culture fit.

Companies must measure the impact of their talent departments both based upon retention, and promotion of new candidates. If there are failures, or disappointments, in the progress made by new employees that fit a trend, or that are hired by a particular recruiter, calibration is required to get to the bottom of any common cause.

Every great company misreads some candidates, hires professional interviewees who make great impressions but bad employees, and misses on a few close calls. But if this task is given the importance it deserves, all in the organization should be aligned about the identifiers of a great candidate.

Social settings are highly underutilized, but fantastic opportunities to observe a prospective employee in an environment that simulates the interactions that might be expected with clients, co-workers and vendors. Assuming an employee does well in the first formal interview, setting a second interview over lunch or dinner and preferably with different folks who might be on that candidate's team, is a great way to evaluate chemistry and emotional intelligence.

A very successful local restaurant chain known for great service uses urgency as part of its interview. Specifically, a host or hostess will advise the interviewing manager that he or she is needed in the kitchen during an interview with prospective wait staff. The manager asks the candidate to follow him, or her, and takes off for the kitchen at a great pace. This is purely an exercise to evaluate the urgency of the prospective employee. If a person is told to follow, and the leader is moving, and the person saunters, one knows something about the importance of urgency in this employee, or at least about that employee's ability to pick up on social cues.

If a business is built upon relationships, brilliant employees who don't make a good first impression, or those who lack a customer service mentality will be a bad fit.

Executive leadership plays a vital role in vetting the first impression skills of new employees, because those leaders often have less exposure to these employees. If a new employee makes a poor first impression in addressing executive leadership, it is incumbent on that leader to question how that employee is likely to impact a client or critical corporate relationship.

A follow up to this point relates to recruiting, leadership, and advancement. If an organization is a truly high performance culture, it will be harder to recruit qualified candidates. Even so, as a general rule, the kinds of employees who thrive in these environments are generally attracted to friends and colleagues with similar ambition and energy levels. The importance of recruiting from within, and creating lucrative incentives for employees to assist in bringing others into the organization cannot be understated.

As it relates to leadership, unless a company is recruiting from another business with a very similar mindset and approach, there will always be challenges with hiring leaders from outside the organization. This is at the heart of incredible growth businesses. They are progressing at a pace others can't hope to match, but the need for more employees and leadership is growing as quickly as the company.

For this reason, high performance growth companies have to alter their approach. One option is for all leaders to start at the reasonable basic level of individual performer, perhaps at a higher salary or with bonus incentives such that the clear understanding of both company and candidate is that the expectation is for candidate to rise to leadership ranks quickly, or the experiment has failed.

In a true meritocracy, quick ascendance into leadership is common, and has the triple benefit of proving the firm is not time and tenure, credibly promoting leaders from within the ranks of performers, and inspiring ambition in all that see promotion is truly possible without someone quitting, getting fired, or retiring.

The second option for an incoming leader in a high performance culture is an apprentice approach, where the incoming lead is connected at the hip to a person doing the job, or a similar job. The new leader must get concentrated exposure to company culture, expectations of leadership, and a sense of precisely how his or her success will be evaluated, (preferably in a way that is tied directly to performance of his or her team).

This includes not only understanding the business with quick mastery of subject matter content, but real opportunity to address and solve team problems and conflicts, so that credibility is being built with the team to be led.

In an alpha driven work culture, plucking a leader from a foreign environment and telling his or her team to simply follow this new person is incredibly challenging both to the team, and to the incoming leader.

An added benefit of the apprentice approach is that if the prospective leader fails, or does not meet company expectations, they never assume the reigns of the team. While the team has been told the expectation may be for the new leader to handle the group, the company's cultural tenants are reinforced even by failure of the leader, as the company sends the message that no single employee is above the mission.

Chapter 8. The Millennial Myth – Separating Hope from Hype

One day or day one. You decide – Paul Coelho

You are supposed to hate millennials. You are supposed to find them to be lazy overgrown teenagers, who live in their parents' homes because of a lack of motivation, and a desire to spend meager expendable income on fancy food and drink. If this is what you go looking for, it is what will be found. The reality is much more complicated.

Time magazine called them lazy entitled narcissists, who still live with their parents. The irony of course is that this magazine and virtually all others have bashed young generations for decades. In 1990, the magazine wrote that the young generation had "trouble making decisions," and said that they would rather hike in the Himalayas than climb a corporate ladder."

Bash the young professionals of the newest generation at your peril. The reality is this. They have been the largest element of the workforce since late 2015. The stereotype that chases this generation has been as aggressive as or more so than the one chasing generation x'ers and their predecessors.

If a growing business does not learn how to attract the lions of this millennial generation, and to fulfill them, it is simply destined to fail.

Lindsey Pollack, is among the most preeminent experts in the subject of millennials in the workplace, and what must be done to maximize their contribution to organizations.

Some of her conclusions are shared by virtually everyone in the field. Millennials cannot thrive in an environment that is lacking in technology. The notion of a reverse mentor has been gaining steam for some time and for good reason.

It works like this. Senior, more experienced, and often older professional leads are paired with a young, ambitious technology enthusiast. The older imparts wisdom from decades of experience. The younger teaches technological relevance. In the end, both get something extremely valuable.

This is not a comment on social media, or the hottest app of the day, although both are vastly more important to business growth than most realize. The reality is that senior corporate leadership is less flexible than it should be in accepting, experimenting with, and applying the incredible tools that current technology brings to bare.

This is true with the technology available for client interaction, whether it be utilization of effective chat bots, or search engine optimization that increases internet traffic.

Pollack has also opined that things such as clarity on career progression, access to leadership, and sense of mission are critical elements to keeping top talent in this younger group known for its willingness to leave a job quickly.

The mistake companies make is in assuming these characteristics to be weaknesses. If the company is seeking lions, and properly recruits them, access to this information with the invitation to make demands even as a new employee, and the earliest of understandings as to how the company makes a difference can all be critical elements in keeping top talent.

The hope is that a fantastic talent will stay for decades when that seems impossible. The hype is that this entire generation can be lumped into a group of lazy foodies, who don't really want to work.

Millennial lions require recognition, and see themselves as individuals. This is true for high performers of every generation. The smartest, most talented, and most ambitions employees in a growth culture will not allow leadership to fail to recognize their genius.

Even so, this generation is like its predecessors in that early celebration of simple victories, without constructive tension, enforcement of culture, and consequences for failure will lead to complacency, and the lack of growth a business requires.

Experience is also paramount to these young professionals. Consider the example set by Zappos, an incredible high performance culture brand. All employees are required to interact with customers, spending time on customer service calls, to ensure an understanding of how the customer, as the lifeblood of the company could be better served.

Boston Beer –known for its premier product Sam Adams, is well known for insisting that all employees, even accountants, love beer first as a preeminent qualification for working there. Why? Because if you love beer, your connection to a high quality beer company will be more than a stiff professional one. It will be personal. It will tie the employee's role to a mission that is admired, and therefore, aligns the employee's interest with those of the company.

Millennials want to get paid, and compensation is critically important in their senses of self, and for recognition. Variety, exposure to the business as a whole through practical experience, apprenticeship, and an environment that promotes leaders who genuinely care about the success of their teams, are all critical here.

Similarly, millennials want to be able to disconnect. They want the Porsche, only if they get the chance to drive it. The balance of personal space, with professional responsibility is one of the great challenges of demanding high performance cultures, seeking talent from the millennial pool.

Communication is also materially different with the newest professional generation. For the first time in history, an educated generation prefers written communication to oral. Consider that for a moment. These are the first employees ever to rely on an emoji to express tone where the human voice previously did so. Take that group, and put them in an environment where emoji's are deemed unprofessional, and the natural reaction can be an awkward toneless exchange of information, and an overreliance on email, where the phone call is a much better solution.

High performance cultures will train millennials through practical examples, and emulation, as to the importance of the human voice, spoken empathy, and verbal communication in the creation of client relationships.

The challenge is that these new employees are still called to communicate with a group that did not use text, email, or social media as a primary means of communication. Perhaps in the future, verbal communication will become increasingly less important, but successful business will recognize that for now, the importance of fluency in both verbal and written communication is paramount.

Feedback has always been important. Many reading these words will recall the stilted, yearly review from a boss, who rarely communicated anything. As an employee there were nerves, apprehension, the not so subtle hope for a raise, and a number of other uncertainties swimming in the minds of the reviewed employee. Millennials may be the first generation to overtly, and properly, reject this approach.

Millennials rightfully require contemporaneous feedback. The notions of Ken Blanchard, who is an incredible genius, in his book The One Minute Manager, have never been more relevant. Spend a minute on the good and a minute on the bad with your millennial employee, and do so regularly.

The result for any talented new hire will be incredible growth, quick mastery, and material contribution to the company's bottom line at light speed. The offshoot is that the employee experience is much improved, and vastly more stable with a team member who knows exactly where she stands at all times.

Chapter 9. What Good Are Caged Lions? – Teaching Your New Talent to Lead

The first responsibility of a leader is to define reality. The last is to say thank you. In between, the leader is a servant – Max DePree

The author here has been blessed to have encountered a wealth of riches as respects leadership.

My most respected leader, and the author of the "my dog died," question described leadership as a "violent act of service." That is extraordinary really in its departure from common notions of the leader as one who gives orders, makes commands and demands, or who otherwise tells subordinates what to do.

The Japanese word Samurai comes from saburai, which means to serve. It is certainly not novel to think of service as a noble act of bravery, given rich traditions of such service. Yet, in the highest performing cultures, an obvious charismatic leader, followed by those with an almost cult-like loyalty is commonplace.

Amongst the most impactful leaders in every context there are those who put their teams before themselves, in obvious and selfless ways. I once asked a millennial marine about his notion of leadership, with full knowledge that I was hiring him for a high growth demanding company filled with young brilliant professionals.

His response got him the job. "In your mind, what does it mean to lead?" I asked. "I see it this way," he said. "My guys ate before me, and they slept before me. They knew I never asked them to do anything I hadn't done or wouldn't do myself, and they were always treated with respect. Because, when the bullets started flying, questions meant lives. Mine, or theirs, or both."

It has often been said that the truest way to know a person is to give them a little money, or power. This notion is cliché because of the fundamental truth at its heart.

I once worked in an environment where team director status was referred to as "Hamburger Hill." The young leaders had a consulting docket of clients for which they were responsible. Upon showing mastery and competence in the field, a newbie or two was awarded to the leader, who maintained responsibility for his or her docket. If there were no glaring problems, this young professional suddenly found themselves in charge of ten professionals, with an ongoing responsibility to continue to take A+ care of that same docket.

Inevitably, the team director would fail miserably, and have it all taken away or quit. The situation became so toxic that new young employees, tried to avoid ascendance into leadership so that they would not face the inevitable.

It is fine to expect young leads to be player/managers. The dual role encourages continued development, and keeps the leaders grounded, while helping to establish credibility as the new folks on the team observe the leader's competence. Even so, leaders must be ever mindful about pushing employees into situations with high likelihood of failure. Simple candor that a person is not yet ready is vastly better, than knowingly placing a young lead in a position that is likely to yield a disastrous outcome.

Strong corporate culture will also invite its performers to lead overtly. Early in my career I can recall working in a fairly dynamic environment where the team was exceptional in some respects with real opportunity for improvement in others. I was hesitant to say anything having been conditioned to a norm that the "new guy," shouldn't come in, and tell those at the organization what to do or how to do it. For some time I kept my head down, did my best to demonstrate the highest competence and work ethic, and expected the rest to take care of itself.

Soon enough, I developed trust in one of the key leaders of the organization, and I was candid with him about my thought that we could do better, and my hesitance to say so. His response was something I will always remember.

"I am watching that group to see who will lead," he said. "I could tell the group who the leader is, in the same way I could point to any dog in a kennel of 30 dogs, and pronounce a brown dog with white spots as the leader. The reality is, the dogs make that decision not me." This was an overt invitation to me to lead, and it gave me a sense of confidence, and personal control over my own career that I had not experienced in other environments.

The converse is also true. I once had a junior leader who was promoted, and retreated to his office isolating himself. He ceased to communicate with his team, and guide them in the way that had led to the promotion in the first place. After a short time, the team began to act on its own. Frustrated, the young manager came to me and said, "they won't follow me."

My response revisited the conversation from above. "Would you have me stand up in front of the group and tell them to follow you, because I command it?" He understood immediately. The only way to get a team to follow is to lead them. Organizations that act as kingmakers, will suffer the consequence of decreased credibility within the ranks, poor performance of teams who do not trust or believe in their leader, and consequently stagnant growth or decline.

So how does an organization heavily dependent on a millennial workforce create that overt invitation to lead, and draw the best from young leaders?

As it turns out, the formula for success here is straightforward. The organization must send the clear message that investment and leadership are the fastest means to elevation within the organization, and all of the rewards that come from it.

These rewards should be reasonably transparent, though I am not a fan of the open book salary trend that seems to be gaining some momentum. The company must make it clear that anyone who performs will have an opportunity to lead, and quickly, and then demonstrate the sincerity of this proposition by identifying performers and giving them the very public chance to lead.

How are those candidates chosen? Nothing can happen before the prospective leader has demonstrated objective competence in the subject matter of the group to be led. While it is true that figurehead leadership, or insertion of leaders from other organizations is commonplace, it is still strained at best, or disastrous at worst if that leader lacks credibility as to competence in the field.

This is doubly so for young leaders, who suffer built in credibility challenges based upon age and life experience.

Leadership instincts, and empathy should be tested by entrusting the leadership candidate to a project that addresses a team need or deficiency. This process involves having the candidate identify the deficiency (an ability critical to any leader). Then the candidate creates a proposal for addressing the situation, with objective identifiable goals and timelines, and that proposal is vetted by the candidate's mentor both for effectiveness of the solution, and the plan for creating team buy in. The candidate is then given the opportunity to execute.

This step must occur before any assignment of a direct report is made, for two reasons. First, it allows the leadership candidate to place themselves in a position of authority with the oversight of the mentor, beginning the path to credibility.

Second, it allows the organization to test the candidate's ability to get buy in, and follow through with the plan created. If a candidate cannot do both of these things well, or if the slightest semblance of power is abused by the candidate, the organization knows that calibration is required and/or can disqualify the leader before entrusting that person with the career of another prematurely.

This path of successful project completion as a means of earning the privilege of developing another should be open and obvious. The chance to develop another should absolutely be seen as a privilege, and the successful development of a culturally aligned high performer by the new leader should be publicly applauded.

As the team grows, mindful discussions about delegation, changes in the proportion of various work assignments, and a transition to schedule driven by more personnel development should occur.

With the assignment of two or three to a new team, project management and the ability to juggle competing tasks should be closely monitored as this is a critical time in the creation of a new leader. Adjustments will be required, but with proper support, a young leader who views the role as an opportunity to serve the team should thrive.

Once the team begins to grow beyond a small cluster, additional scrutiny is required. Many performance organizations use a "360 review" process or similar analytical tool to evaluate readiness of a new leader to take on a larger team.

The 360 analysis involves anonymous feedback about the leader (often conducted in the form of open ended question surveys by a third party administrator). The feedback is sought from the leader's supervisors, peers, and subordinates. As a leader ascends in any organization the ability to manage concerns and issues both up and down within the organization becomes increasingly important, and the visibility of that leader to others in the organization gives the company additional lenses through which to evaluate progress.

By far the most important feedback for the small team lead comes from the team itself. One hopes that in a transparent culture team members feel comfortable providing constructive feedback even to leaders, but this is simply not always the case.

If anonymous feedback from the team shows glaring deficiencies in the leader, or worse an unwillingness of the team to follow the leader, the process of advancement must stop until these issues are addressed.

Promotion of a leader to a place of higher authority without peer and subordinate buy in is toxic. Unchecked, such promotion can quickly undermine the corporate goal of meritocracy, by creating the impression that favoritism, or subjective popularity drives advancement and not performance.

There are hundreds of books on leadership technique, and this is not intended to displace any of them. Instead, the goal is to provide a simple, executable approach to promotion that speaks to the needs of young leadership candidates in any organization.

Chapter 10. What Do They Say? – Millennials in Their Own Words

First, we never refer to ourselves as millennials - Every person on Earth born between 1980 and 2000.

Is the term "millennial" derogatory? In as much as any label, can become a lazy overly general descriptor, one could argue the case that it is. It is certainly true that a number of people born within the period traditionally associated with the word millennial abhor the designation, and connect it to unfair stereotypes that don't get to the heart of who these folks are as individuals.

On the other hand, virtually all generations have some descriptive moniker. Generally the older generation admires its accomplishment of incredible things despite adversity, and operates from a position of the power afforded by experience and accumulated wealth. One could go back hundreds of years and look at how older people describe youth, and if the dates were hidden from the reader, similarities would be uncanny despite vast changes in culture and circumstance.

Even so, there are characteristic environmental factors that play a critical role in understanding the perspective of any generation. One cannot separate the baby boomer from the times of conflict and prosperity they experienced.

Similarly, for the millennial generation unprecedented access to information, and material changes in communication norms brought on by social media and technology cannot be ignored. There is a substantial body of work that seeks to better understand this critically important group in that context, but much can be learned from simply listening to them.

For one thing, this group rarely refers to themselves as millennials. Whether this is a function of the desire to maintain individuality in the way that is all too important especially in youth, or whether it is a function of the perception that other generations use the word millennial in a pejorative way, know that this word can be loaded with unintended meaning.

Millennials have had unprecedented access to, and therefore dependence on, technology. Workplaces that seek to be havens of new young talent must take this into consideration both in terms of the tools made available to employees, but also as it relates the expectations communicated to employees.

The use of certain written and communication conventions that are normal amongst our youth can appear unprofessional, or even disrespectful to others as described in previous chapters.

When surveyed, millennials place a much higher emphasis on experience than their parents did, and much lower emphasis on earning. Survey after survey bears this out.

The importance of such research is that companies seeking high performers from this generation cannot take for granted that money is the only thing motivating the workforce. To the contrary, many millenials report that the importance of the mission, the work environment, and how they are treated on the job in terms of recognition and flexibility are more important than the amount of compensation.

Similarly, other measures such as company access to fitness facilities, yoga or cooking classes, and other experience based perks may yield much better retention than the same dollars invested in salaries could buy.

Companies that place an emphasis on their care for the health and wellbeing of employees through such offerings also experience improvements to the bottom line in health insurance savings, increased productivity, and decreased employee absenteeism.

Even within the ranks of those born in the last 20 years of the 1900's there are material differences depending upon other factors. For example, in a large survey of millennial employees from 2017, Deloitte discovered that young people in emerging markets are twice as likely as their mature market counterparts of the same age to have optimism about their financial and emotional wealth relative to that of their parents.

Companies that want to attract the cream of this crop would do well to show prospective candidates their own commitment to improving the lives of new employees in creative ways.

Millennials report a much closer kinship to the younger generation, which has been called generation z among other things. Similarities in upbringing, dependence upon technology, and views on the world as a whole have been argued by commentators as a kind of glue binding these generations together. The takeaway there is that additional effort is required to bridge communication and experience gaps between millennials and their older counterparts.

In terms of social obligation, millennials describe their obligations to others in much more global terms than their parents did.

Despite a reputation for sloth which is hotly contested, millennials tend to be very active in volunteering locally, but are much more likely both to be aware of, and to assist those in need in other countries with causes that are close to their hearts.

Social progress, or the lack thereof is a much more likely criticism when millennials talk about their nations' leaders, than the criticisms offered of older generations that tend to be more focused on monetary, and security concerns.

What does this mean for leaders of high performance cultures dependent on millennials? Harvest the energies of these folks better by allowing flex time that helps the social image of the brand, while building connectivity with employees who want to make a difference.

Final Thoughts

In some ways, leadership of the modern corporate world is more obvious than it has ever been. The ability to embrace change, constructive tension, and abandonment of formalities for sincere honesty coming from a place of genuine concern can give any ordinary person the incredible power of leadership.

That conclusion is probably not new, but the recognition that employees have a power to demand of their employer is. Loyalty in the form of the career worker that stays with a company for decades seems like a pipe dream. Then again, the promise of a company that will take care of you in your old age, because you took care of it in your youth, will always seem like a bargain.

The company that offers engaging challenging work, stimulating interaction with smart talented people, and access to a gym to combat stress with the goal of a healthy body and spirit will always have an advantage.

Our leaders now must fundamentally ignore some of the advice of their parents. Don't keep your head down. Do confidently confront weaknesses in your organization. Kindness for its own sake can lead to weakness, and the rejection of passivity will repel mediocrity.

Young people are not easily hemmed in by stereotypes, and the intelligent selection of lions among lambs will guarantee a disruptive force that protects the growth of the company through innovation.

The moment you set this book down, as a leader in any organization, you should begin to consider what you will demand of those around you, and where your company is weak.

Those who love the company will embrace any who try to shore it up. Phrases like "we have always done it this way," should fill you with a sense of disgust.

There should be an introspective consideration of every leader in the company that asks "why him, or her?" If the answer is anything but investment in others, calibration is a priority.

I will never forget the words of a young engineer in my consulting firm who told me this:

> When I started here, I went to my father and told him how excited I was about who we are, and what we are doing. At first he nodded politely. When I was still as excited at six months, and then a year he took me to the side.
>
> He told me that he remembered being a young engineer at a small but thriving company that was innovative, exciting, and incredibly rewarding. The company became massive, and then slowly, it was as if the colors faded. Soon it wasn't about designing impossible products, or changing the world. It was about where to go for lunch, and what happened over the weekend. My father told me that if I cared about this place I worked, I would be diligent to ensure that the colors never faded.

I have always loved this simple example of wisdom exchanged between a father and his son. It isn't at all the story of fading colors. It is a simple and sad reflection on what causes the death of great organizations. This is, of course, completely avoidable. The question is, what are you going to do about it?

www.ingramcontent.com/pod-product-compliance
Lightning Source LLC
Chambersburg PA
CBHW070304230526
45470CB00002B/715